AN IMPRINT OF WHAT BOOKS PRESS | LOS ANGELES

ALSO BY JUDITH PACHT

COLLECTIONS
Summer Hunger
Infirmary for a Private Soul

CHAPBOOKS
Falcon
User's Guide
A Cumulus Fiction
St. Louis Suite

PRECARIOUS

PRECARIOUS

NEW & SELECTED POEMS

Judith Pacht

Library of Congress Cataloging-in-Publication Data

Names: Pacht, Judith author
Title: Precarious : new & selected poems / Judith Pacht.
Other titles: Precarious (Compliation)
Description: Topanga, CA : Giant Claw, 2025. | Summary: "These poems ask us
   to consider our own personal struggles with morality. As we choose
   whether to respect the traffic light's turn from red to green, whether
   to flaunt the law nor not, at every turn we face challenges inside,
   outside. Many are precarious"-- Provided by publisher.
Identifiers: LCCN 2025030400 | ISBN 9798998905520 paperback
Subjects: LCGFT: Poetry
Classification: LCC PS3616.A3285 P74 2025
LC record available at https://lccn.loc.gov/2025030400

Cover art: Gronk, *Untitled*, 2024
Book design by ash good, www.ashgood.com

Giant Claw
363 South Topanga Canyon Boulevard
Topanga, CA 90290

GIANTCLAWPRESS.COM

For Ken

CONTENTS

SELECTED POEMS

NEW POEMS

You are looking outwards, and that above all things you should avoid right now. There is but the one remedy: go within.

—RAINER MARIA RILKE, *Letters to a Young Poet*

Be yourself; everyone else is already taken.

—OSCAR WILDE

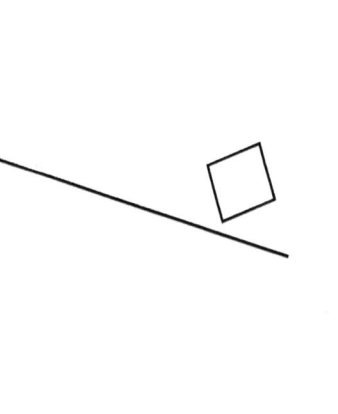

ANOTHER NEW POEM

after Charles Wright

It will meet evasive eyes.
It will be variously orbited, placed.
It will speak what is not spoken.

It will expose shifting decoys.
It will face the bleak unknown.
It will console our Selves.

It will heal hidden wounds.
It will change fear to insight.
It will birth another new poem.

LIBERA ME

The faint trace of skunk
far from sirens & congestion—
steer manure, leaf-change, earth-scent.
Allow me more: to scout out dry husks, wet soil,
to feel mid-day peels, white-breath nights.
Dark-mined mornings with my doves & squirrels
mark the month's near end. Next year this time late
fall again. Dark days. *Libera me, Domine.*
Faure seduces by opening doors, but where
to go through, how or why? Maybe
self-correction or change of course.
His *Libera Me,* freedom through death, tempts—but
I inhabit life, learn from love & rage.
Learn from seeing blind.

ABE THE TILE MAN

fixes a split
he works with
thought   corrects

warped   broken
roof lines   broken
tiles

it takes a while   to make
the crooked straight
to fill the spaces inbetween

repair is solace for
        a split   a hurt

repair saves heart
                I mean

is it enough

to try to erase   correct
enough to make
the rough places plain

THE VOICE OF THE FROG

you have to start early
listen hard   stand still
in the doorway

insistent familiar
hidden in lavender
           his voice

knows my footstep
or is it my shadow

      who owns this pond?

as I pass

I know him only by his rough
                 call
just outside my wall
        of doors

      this water is mine

I do not know him really
he grows silent
      any strange
      change of light

cuts the black air   erases
traffic   nightjars   crickets
in the darkening

I cut the air with self re
crimination   re
creation of

what was said   unsaid
done   left undone

BBC SHIPPING FORECAST, FACING SOUTH

precarious   when my view south
looks back at me   & as for place
(say it)   a part of me looks down
& in   trying to avoid visibility

it's me   my self   & as for place
occasionally
I don't avoid visibility
facing south

on the other hand   sometimes
north is more precise
I know how shame lies
in & down   know to avoid south-facing
                                        visibilities

though north seems more precise
                              occasionally
squalls   the gales cyclones   shudders
in & down   I can't avoid
the variable (sometimes poor) visibility

squalls   gales   that shudder again

look down

shame looks back at me   me   the self
& that precarious facing

ON CONSCIENCE

Wrong: an early imprint on the self,
Dark & weighty, sullen as a stone
That ducks & reappears as something else,
As if to change that imprint of oneself.
Something else must break through dark to Yes,
Open doors, leave No & No alone,
Instead hear Yes & Yes imprint itself,
No longer weighty, sullen as a stone.

*

What was it that I did at four or five?
I pulled out ringlets, strands of her red hair
(Those watery eyes, pale freckled skin) besides
What did I know when I was four or five
Playing house just in the yard outside.
She took away my doll which wasn't fair
But what is fair when one is four or five?
So I pulled out some strands of her red hair.

*

There's more:
I've stolen now & then, one time a peach
Another time a word, an hour. Yes & No
Sit far apart, withheld, alive in silent speak.
Still, thieving can be sweet (think ripened peach,
Think open doors) the boundaries so oblique
One word, one hour, rescues me from *No.*
So stealing now & then, a word, one peach,
A slice of heart (yours, mine) may be right
                                        & wrong.

13

PERSONAL TRUTH, TWO STORIES

i.
Briney: Mother & her Manhattan clam chowder,
shellfish & caraway seeds, tomatoes—not Boston cream.
Fall & Spring, stews & soup. Rain. Wild winds
sweep 114th Street uphill to Broadway,
sting eyes, wet my fat cheeks. I hug the buildings,
familiar streets talk me safe at dark or do they?
Mother's disappeared. What's left:

                    my feigned independence.

ii.
In 2024 the film *This Time Next Year*

                    is playing.
Remember   the Prophet Elisha said to Sarah
Next year at this time you will have a child—at 91.
Millennia span from Bible to screen—the plot,
a connecting thread.
The movie invents as does the Bible as do I.
Pick your fiction.

A FRACTIONAL BALANCE

just now
he was leaning
on our door   sugar grains
stuck to his lips, popping cherry
gum drops

a joke   this memory
from another life
one where he shoved
through crowds   flung a dare
& it soft-landed

*

forbidden: jostling on the gangplank as you disembark

*

a fractional balance   this sliver
of blue air   regrets
flying   no time for last
                        words

our lips move
soundlessly   eyes shrouded
faces folded as crumpled metal cans
crushed

          & every Wednesday
          the trash gets collected

PORTRAIT

I say inner beauty doesn't exist. That's something that unpretty
women invented to justify themselves. —Osmel Sousa

She has excised
what some call
excess
        an ever so slight
        fat-flap at the waist
        a prominent nose
        her pointed chin
                pain + time
                her currency
leaves her
        longing
for something unseen
        searching
deep reaches   back
        to that dim corner
        where she (privately)
        turns over   arranges   rearranges
                        pieces
        a portrait   from shattered reflections
           in a convex mirror
           looking for anything that might be
                proof
        (it must be there)
        of her worth.

DEPENDING ON THE YEAR,
A BROKEN PANTOUM

A word is only what it means
old love   white noise   round sounds
titillate at night   in daylight
fractured as old skin   fault-lined

a love that was   white noise   round sounds
my tongue tries to say the words
fautltlines again   *did I write that   say that*
yes   here it is

my tongue is trying   still not a poem
& the passion's not quite gone
yes here it is   the likeness doesn't scan
my edit-eye excises sentiment

allows some passion   (his receding chin)
a taste of past   Selma's cake with plums
my edit-eye   my tongue remembers
cold-sweet   warm-tart   enjambed as lovers' limbs

those plums in Selma's cake
sharp   intense   but flat   depending on the year
cold-sweet   warm-tart   enjambed as lovers' limbs
despite my private fears

sharp   intense & flat   depending on the year
but colored wild & rapturous   ravenous
despite our private fears
words aren't only what they mean

DEPRESSION SOUP, 1936

grasses tuck
    slivered duck
    scallions   in bao-clouds
orders sing out
          loud
      vowels
treble clatter
      roll & rattle
      metal carts at Sammy Yee's

right here
mother ladles
soup pot to bowl
          noodles
    tangle
    mounds
    of ancient
hens' feet
broth leached & leached   hours & hours
from barely bubbling bones

father's bald head
a brass-globed finial
    gleams tall over
    suit & tie
starched dinners

mother's ordered breaths   Her Table
    set for dining

with me   an animal
                   whose procreant urges:
                             primal   ravenous
                 suck jellied bits off
      mount of moon
      mount of Venus
my hands
    their feet

ABOUT CHARGED BODIES

with a line from Carl Dennis

in the world of the subjunctive
if you think about imbalance or

      attachment

      about bodies
      about polar opposites that
         attract   attach

                 attack

think of
charged bodies
moving at the speed of light

if they

    would resist
    the traveling current

    and

    (ignoring what
    could be grounding
        thinking only about

        imbalance   attaching   attacking)

know that earthing busbars
can ground current & volts

know you can open refuge

then
  (are you listening?)

        the world of the imperative
        could change your life

PRECARIOUS

February 5, 2025

we raked
the decomposed
granite smooth
                but
decomposed again
it cracked
when the earth
shook

in Fort Worth
I remember   soundless black
massing around me
the tornado's vortex

                precarious
as
this wildfire   hot
enough to melt
my car's metal   flat
onto the asphalt

today   a red light
flashing
        reads *stop* to many

                others proceed
                deceive
                say it again & again: *red is green*

I write this
because it's my truth:
        guard the flashing red

THE POET AT FOUR

The chalk, the sidewalk, her unsteady hand
scratched a line, looped a loop with hair,
drew wobbly Js & later vowels (unplanned)
turned into names with consonants to spare.

No one really noticed, did they,

when fresh images & words surprised, see-
sawed
inside her head: landscapes, a tree, a curse,
a verse
in *Hochdeutsch,* Grandfather's language.

She wet her finger to the wind
leaned into disconnect
fancied insight, depth,
& played with shock, her newest toy,

cut the slightest slant, forbade the tonal fugue,
declined to rhyme.

UNTIED

scraps collected
saved & shaped to stanzas
or laid out with care on paper
like starched & ironed organza
                              crushed
            oh those crumpled hours
            torn & tossed away
                        (something might be there)

                  & then   once when I was three
I tried to tie my shoe   hurled it flying
                  fury against the flowered wall paper
                  making bruises of purple-petaled flowers

not so much later
I came to know
            the shoe's lace better
                        its loop-the-loop
                        its up-round-down
& then the lace & I
            became a bow

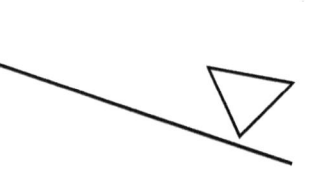

ANOTHER SLOW FADE

in memory of JP
after Ishiguro's Klara and the Sun

lingering papercut-cruelties
                    or tenderness

& abandonment again

        you know how it goes
        one gone & one left
        plunged into orphanhood

affecting the same absence
of person   wisdom & smart-ass repartee

        as alpenglow fades & disappears

                in every direction

        unwashed dishes   disheveled sheets
        two fishing boots each molded by a foot

his body heat
not erased   simply
        (think Verdi's *Va Pensiero*)

a pulse
a heart   whole & beating
        that outlives us

25

PORTA PORTESE

Because it is Rome. Because Jerry died seven months ago. Friends warn *beware of Italian men*. Bits & pieces reassemble the unfocused kaleidoscope inside my head. And look! There is Porta Portese nearby, a welcome distraction and favorite haunt, but today holds only a few more hours. My time in Rome is short.

Using arms and head gestures an autobus driver directs me toward a nearby street, the Grand Via. Another bus stop and a short walk later, another autobus. This driver nods *Si, Porta Portese*.

A small cadre has followed me to help, gesturing, talking rapid Italian and by now every prospective autobus passenger knows my destination. Sitting in the last row I try to focus, remember the map I studied, unscramble the streets leading to the market. I don't know where to get off or which streets lead to which streets. A gray haired man in a tweed jacket with a blue checked shirt has heard me ask about Porta Portese.

And then, at last. *Si, si* my cadre-chorus calls out *Porta Portese!*—the man in tweed waves to me. I have forgotten be wary as he and I stroll towards the market stringing together bits of French, my fractured Italian, his good English. *Where are you from*, he asks, *how long are you here, do you know of Montova?* Footsteps, halting phrases, silences. *Are you a professor?* I am not. Gesturing to his ring and then mine he asks, *are you married?* I nod, move in this new direction with a newly pleasant calm, our quiet walk. *Si, my husband died in April,* I say.

Unpredictable, uncontrollable, a void opens. I try every trick, everything I know to stop the tears. *Scusa,* the man says to me. *No, no—m'scusa,* I say. We pass stalls of dusty shoe leather, mounds of brilliant orange tomatoes, purple *carciofi* of all sizes, conversational diversions, every one. I beg myself to stop.

The unlucky man walks quietly next to me until at last I am composed. Porta Portese's stalls and a swirl of shoppers sprawl around us in all directions.

We're here, he gestures. My hand reaches out to shake his, determined to reappear as he's met me, self-assured & now grateful, but my hand remains mid-air. He gently embraces me, kissing each cheek once, then returns to the first cheek. A shower of Italian, a smile & he disappears into the crowd, his ultimate kindness making all that came before seem ordinary, completely natural, a matter of course.

THERE—NOT THERE

You're there—not there. Just inside the sage-green door. Shadows, an odd disquiet. Here's the razor-sharp knife; you knew how to brace the steel & feel for nuanced nicks, so faint I can only intuit their absence. We pressed the perfect crust into the fluted pan, baked the perfect pie imperfectly, listened to the errant boom-box you tuned. It drifted band to band. Now pencil lines on masking tape mark music, news, our game of find it keep it no more left to chance. No more chants drift past my breakfast toast—

> *. . . can't travel*
> *away from you*
>
> *rolling pine cone*
>
> *each time I go to leave*
> *my shoes hide*
> *in your dreams . . .*

& in the pantry under the green glass bottle of *Vinho Verde* resting sideways on the shelf, under the sagging paper bag of tortillas, behind the cracked plastic bucket (useless now), traces of a mouse.

NOTES FROM THE EDGE
IN THE TIME OF COVID

January 5, 2021

inside our carapaces
we waterbreathers
oyster-like

briny-bellied & languid
      hang
on in shallow water
in breaking surf
our muscled/feet hold

but know to inch away
know how to close our shells
      tight

FABLE ON ERASURE

after Nazim Hikmet, A Fable of Fables

We stand at the source,
This dirt path & me.
Fog & sleet disguise
The hedge, the stones.
Daylight with no light.
Fog masks the dirt path.

We stand at the source,
This dirt path twists the cold & me.
Fog & sleet veil
Hedge, stones.
Daylight but no light, moves not seen.
Fog masks the twisted, the walls, the stones.

We stand at the source,
This twisted dirt path & me,
                    cold, stones. No sun.
Fog & sleet hide
What's stolen: hedge, stones, part of me.
Daylight with no light
Erases theft, the twisted path, the cold, the hedge
                    & me.

We stand at the source,
Fog and sleet erase
Path & memory,
My voice, his & hers, yours, stolen.
Stones & hedge, sound & voice gone.
No sun allowed, voices not allowed,
Not one.

WITHOUT: LOS ANGELES, APRIL 2020

As though dishes from the Veneto
could fade to shades of gray, purple fruited
flowers seep away, outlines faint,
their fluted borders smooth.

As though a skillet caramelizing apples
(in perfect slices), sugared, overlapping,
sautéed without one lick of tongue
could taste bitter underneath the sweet.

Or, lip-reading *Libera me Domine,*
one could imagine Fischer-Dieskau's baritone
spacious but unheard, Faure's *Requiem*
dead-silent—yet every note scored.

Where is the acrid scent of burning leaves
in red & yellow piles? Hunger for
the language of a season telegraphing
colors, gusts, cold air

as though our bodies could forget cold
when heat still wraps our bones. Can they unlearn
fingers tracing the hollows in a face.
How distance chills.

The hills & fields are poppy-orange!
Pollen-drugged I taste young shoots, bruised blooms,
remember the taste of skin, the scent.
Yours. I'm ravenous.

HUMMINGBIRD

how close
how far
we go
              the hummingbird
& me
     our wingfeather trills

ruled by hunger
or fear
      the balance
      teeters

      beaks

     (hoverbird's
& mine) search for a scintillant

  wingbeat   a heartbeat
      to keep us
      hovering

close   but not too close
distant   but not too distant

     always

      longing

ELEGY FOR A
FORGOTTEN LANDSCAPE

not unleavened bread
not thickening stratus nimbus clouds
                    tempting rain
                    to scour my landscape clean
                    the scent of after-rain

not honest thorns & cactus   clumps of chamisa
                    the howl of a coyote in the dark

instead
                    two-story columns
                    three-story houses block after block
                        each built to the lot-line

                            bathrooms & bathrooms
                            bedrooms & bedrooms

        rolls of callow turf   ready to roll
        green blades   each exactly cut
        1-1/2 half inches tall

                        a broken history
                        of what used to be

A FAR REACH

for Stuart & Beverly

bushwhacked
& no sea breeze

humid   stifling
the uphill hike

a consolation
this shaded cave   I shed
layers down to my skin
curl up   nap
                cool at last

that's luck if you can find it

        circular as infinity

as when Stuart
cleaned the krater

& out fell millennia
the remains
of a snake
    coiled   translucent
    intact

        tail in his mouth

call it magic
my friend said of death
a *uroboros*

34

I call it a portent

this changing form
            a protection
reaching deep into the past

Note: I've arranged the Selected Poems not by the book in which they originally appeared, but in conversation with each other over time. For readers wishing to know the book the poem first appeared in however, the book's title is noted at the right-hand bottom of the page.

SELECTED POEMS

Consider how archaeologists approach
finding shards and fragments, bit by bit.

—YVONNE RAND

THE CORE BALANCE TRAINER

touches your hard-to-reach center,
subdues the imbalance that rises
from the belly some days, ballast
for those moods that weigh & shift, those lurches,
though there are times
when even the non-skid tread deep inside

skids

oblique as abdominal muscles,
your core balance slips away,
pitching and yawing
like the boom
of a gaff-rigged schooner
coming about in an uncertain wind.

Summer Hunger

SURFACE

Like a motel, the table by the bed,
the dressers, veneer, everything
matching, serene and restful as motels
are meant to be, for the business traveler
who clinches a merger, the hungry lovers
who clinch and merge,
the invisible room
service, the waiter's smile as he enters
each opened door,

although you know, some days
with an ear to the facing, you can hear
the plywood peeling strip by strip,
the glue melting, dissolving to liquid,
and in a wind the water roils oily black
or turns viscous, even tears the heart,
all the while the veneer's shining smooth,
the grain unmarked,

and who would know, or even care, unless you prized
something solid, durable, unless you counted on it.

Summer Hunger

40

WATERVILLE, MAINE,
NEAR GREAT POND

There were woods, there were winters, summers and a girl
lying under the elm. She was ten, a new watch on her wrist.
This was enough, this was everything.
She lay on peat from fallen leaves, her cushion of ten times ten.

She was lying under the elm, a new watch on her wrist
the scent of resin and damp earth, musk and bark in the air,
her cushion of ten times ten from fallen leaves
thick and brown from years of slow-melting snow.

The scent of resin and damp earth, musk and bark hung in the air.
That day sun licked the elm leaves, licked her eyelids
as she lay on powdered leaves, thick from slow-melting snow.
A gentle wind stirred the air soft over shallows on Great Pond.

That day sun licked the elm leaves, licked her eyelids—
though something she couldn't reach flickered by.
Wind stirred the air soft over shallows on Great Pond
where she always swam, right over there.

Something she couldn't reach flickered by
and she thought of the sun pressing early spring to summer,
warming where she swam—right over there
where the lazy traffic of birds, a breeze, shook the elm.

As though the sun is pressing early spring to summer, she thought.
This is enough: the breeze, the elm, the lazy traffic of birds.
There were woods, there were winters, summers in those days.
She set her new watch to keep that time. Ten. She was ten that day.

Summer Hunger

KIN

On a coffinlike
table tethered
by plastic straps,
a leash of sorts,
I think of Howie
the spaniel-eyed mutt
         now mine
caged last week
at the animal shelter.

      He was panting
      nose quivering
      not decoding
      strange sounds,

           pings & bangs
           that speak
           in tongues.

An artificial breeze
pretends fresh air
inside my carapace,
a mirror flirts with
the ceiling/sky,
the technician's room.

The room's there, not
           there.

A hollow
voice in my ear
instructs
    Breathe even breaths.
    Instructed I clench a plastic rod
    between my teeth.

    At home Howie worries a plastic bone.

The technician
one room away
talks to the nurse
ever so faintly.

I hear him say,
    When I ask her
    a question
    she barks back at me.

Infirmary for a Private Soul

THE DEAL

No one pulls her—
She goes willingly,
enjoys the bruises

on her upper arm
under the blue shirt,
reveres his mind,

the smile, the tongue
that reels off history:
Plutarch's *Advice*

to Married Couples,
Constantine's Sword.
The show of intellect

turns her on, She'll promise
anything when he talks
mean or smart, scares her

on the Autostrade swerving
through a soggy stretch
locals call the Styx.

She lives with hell
and likes it,
his three-headed habits

dropping clothing everywhere,
stacking dirty dishes with the clean,
She won't reveal the third.

Meanwhile
he comes and goes
no questions asked,

which works for her
as long as she can take
the ride—oh, how she loves

the ride—from Vicenza
along the river
to see the villas

of Palladio,
as long as she can
suck the sweet-tart juice

of pomegranate seeds.

Summer Hunger

FALCON

Dunnsmuir, Scotland

Never mind *diurnal,* I know

you seize the day, calculate
fly-time to the fraction

of a wink, those unblinking

gold-flecked eyes
measure the hare's gait

from half a mile. Wing-swing, dive,

thunderbolt of notched beak
quick to the back, snapping it.

It's what you dream at night I want to know,

how sleep hones precision:
below, the darkened field of oil seed rape

or gorse, the tremble of a stalk,

the twitching ears, the scurry.
You know the carrion's mind or spine,

how to break each one

precisely—a kind of nocturnal
practice for a clean kill

—not sport, not

human fantasies
splayed,

hooded black

or red on a concrete floor
like those, say,

in Abu Ghraib.

Summer Hunger

SIDEWINDER

I walk the Albuquerque Road
wherever I am.

Wetlands fool you for a while
but the desert wind rises reckless in clear blasts,
flattens you in flares of heat.

>Today the sand is wind-whipped,
>blows, quiets itself, lies rippling
>head low as a snake half-hidden,
>
>though   he is here—the lip
>that yesterday seemed
>safe enough, today snaps,
>
>tight as a sewn seam,
>hollow tooth hidden under his skin,
>the J mark-bruise on mine spells
>
>Judith. Right here. From the rim
>of his blue eye
>a dark cheek-stripe skims
>
>to his mouth   and I'm
>struck, blindsided.
>To think I'd given him
>
>my life, my own
>and for all those years a home.

I ask, *Do we have a plan for Thursday night,*
or *What about the biopsy?*
To the tongue of the blind *ask* means *provoke.*

Yes. I used to think that was love.   *Summer Hunger*

UNDELIVERED MOTHERS DAY

My cabbage rose is drooping from the sun,
her petals opened full, a bit undone
like any dowager -- by heat noon-day
when fading parts or petals drop away.

Her scent commands the air larger than blooms
as if to say, *I'm settled in my room
on flowered beds of chintz*, her color high,
a shade of purple-pink like dusk and sky.

No demure tea-rose she who in her youth
disdained the freesia's fragrance as uncouth.
My cabbage rose protects herself with thorns
from intimacy, perceived weakness scorned.

A grand dame ever ever to the end,
her dignity forbids her stalk to bend.

Infirmary for a Private Soul

ON THE DRESSER

Green stem
erect in a glass,
tulip sepals taut
over petals, the bud
                    a promise.

Call it shy for now
                    or arch,
there's a certain reserve

but the bloom's warm
skin implies
something more

has elapsed. Days,
peach-colored heat,
wet air

& the petals half-open
        as lids
        after deep sleep.

The stalk tips,
anthers slim & dark
bend & blink.

Call it modesty,
a slow revelation.

One morning
        or is it afternoon—
slanted sun
hits the dresser

& it doesn't matter anymore.

The stem
doubles over
    petals widen,
    a footstep sets
    the wanton orange flesh

                trembling.

A shadow memory
of petals falling, the feeling of letting go.

Infirmary for a Private Soul

INSIDE TALLGRASS PRAIRIE

As if

the spaces
between clumps between
deergrass spikes

must
have always
been here

lying with leaf-fall
in the scrub-gray field
deadstill, unseen.

Not
    stab & rustle,
    trampled stalks,
    a scent of crush.

Instead

    inside nothing
    something
could give breath, make room

for the unperceived,
the unexpected.

Call it want, desire
            without

wild wind   or heat.

Infirmary for a Private Soul

THE DREAM

I don't love you as if you were salt-rose or topaz... —Pablo Neruda

I don't love you as if you were salt-rose or topaz,
each one only an imitation of elegance.
The salt-rose petals edge themselves in chalk,
masquerading damask flowers, discreet and pale

as sea air—their ragged blooms look best
at a distance like that other dissembler,
topaz. Not amber or diamond, it seems glass
but calls itself yellow sapphire, a pretender.

No, I love you because you let your hair
go grey, for your humor, raucous or dry,
for warm body nights, cold air, your scent of musk,

your even breaths in sleep, a dream we've told
each other deep and bottomless, one
that's real as life and growing old.

Summer Hunger

BIRD

A slice of sheep cheese with apple ...

you were saying
when the window shook

—or was it the whole wall—
and on the ground a wren,

beak and needle talons
in barest motion,

obsidian eyes
dazed, fooled by light

seeming air, seeming
endless as sky.

Who hasn't flown
too fast and high,

song full
in the belly

sun-warm after a rain,
the sweet taste

dazzling. Sometimes
it ends this way,

a blind fracture
after a moment

of so much
so complete,

that fullness under
wild-streaked feathers.

Feel her, she's still warm.

SPIDER

She hangs

between
    drywall & cement,
    floor & painted wall
    inside her tangled mess

resting.
    Belly up & naked,
    private parts
        exposed,

her crimson birthmark
calls out
her name.

I wonder if she's weary,
    her day filled
    spinning,
          fetching a silk taste,
               a fly-by,
caught in a cycle, spinning.

Me,
    I scoop lint
    from the dryer, weather
    strip a leaky window,

quotidian comforts
      can kill what's precious,

both of us
        intimate assassins
                spinning

to cover
        death's dark cheek,
        his scratch & stubble,

        the ink-black deep
                iris in his eye.

Infirmary for a Private Soul

A VIOLENCE OF SEASON

Cold drops like a hawk
on Blue Hill, Maine.
It bores into the skin, the heart,
claws the eye.

She craves and fears
the imprint of weather:
piles of leaves waiting
for a ceremony of scented smoke,
the shrinking day, the sun's
oblique afterthought, cool on rooftops.
The stubbled field. A lace of frost.

She longs for rain to freeze,
to blow dark and sideways,
smack the barn broadside
smack the back, drape the limbs
of staggering trees.

Behind   gray rubs gray   the horizon spare as a pencil line.

*

At last the fat-cheeked bulbs spring shoots.
And then, ear close to the earth,
She hears their damp breath, watches
for the yellow-wild iris to feather,
the birch and oak to bud.

*

On Narragansett's shore
a fractured moon marks the tides,

tracks the dunes' drifts and hollows.
She hunts clams in the wet sand
where the shallows ebb.
Fingers water-puckered toes
feeling for the quahog's shell
treading fast and deep.

*

She craves and fears the fever of August,
the airless weight of it on the briny pond, the serpentine.
August, the month her daughter rested on her belly,
cord attached—shared blood, shared heat.
This newborn warm,
she still remembers warm.

Her girl, legs long as a filly, temper short,
barefoot in the roundup against the war, barefoot
at the police station, sandals swinging, hair swinging,
broad mouth, broad smile, conscience wide
and deep

gone with summer

in this violence of season,
as cold claws at the eye, shudders,
drops like a hawk.

Jane Siegel
August 8, 1955–August 2, 1972

Summer Hunger

LANDSCAPE WITH TRICKSTER

He stands
at the homesteader's door,
crumbling straw-laced clay walls around him,
looks back

as through a viewfinder,

pulls from the view
a shining dirt floor
smooth, cool to the sole.

Across the Rio Grande
a far bank of sand,
a scattering of low adobes.

      Someone's cracking
      pinons with his teeth
      at a kitchen table.
           It is you
    gone

      fourteen years and two months
      and it is you, still using your mouth
      to conquer a small corner of the world.

         I say your name, hear
         your voice rumble past me

unconnected.

I want to know,
are you whole?
Alone?

Do you have your meds,
how do you fill
the emptiness?

A wild mustang roaming free,
you are saying,
an unbridled equus.

CIRCLE

Julia is losing clumps of hair. She wears a wig out in the world, but at home or on long walks the wig stays hidden on her vanity. Plunging into cool deep shade, her gray brown strands scatter under branches. Mulch thickens from years of leaves & rain. She settles into a drift of loss to contemplate chemotherapy. The air a chorus of cicadas, birdsong, the winged zzz of diving insects. One tree limb rubs against another. Nothing is here, everything is here: spider silk & moss for nests, leaves for hatching swallowtail butterflies, the occasional cloud that darkens. Two birds circle. She watches them disappear into a thicket with her thin strands in their bills, strands to line their nest, shape their home.

Infirmary for a Private Soul

CT ABDOMEN:
WITH & WITHOUT I-V CONTRAST

We worried that boys would see through our flimsy voile dresses (how we loved their cling) worried our nipples—or something more—might show. We wanted boys to see through the flimsy voile but not all the way to the barely healed scars, the wounded feelings, the way we were oh so much less than, though we acted so much more than—talked of Albee & Beckett, not a lot but as though. Later the boys came breath-close & they tasted our hearts. It was not easy.

Given the choice today, Wednesday, I'll take my CT scan neat without contrast, & this time please, skip the evidence of flaw now posted public knowledge on X-ray & Findings.

Another December Wednesday & the canopy of deep green, a windless blizzard of sharp points flecking, falling, the scatter of splinters, my giant camphor tree dispatched. Only a medicinal scent & pink-fleshed chips remain. Oak Root Fungus silently ate the roots that fed & held it for fifty years. Orange-vested men grind its limbs to bits, suck them up the chute, haul them off. It's winterwarm, good for growing fungus underground. There's algae in the pond's yellow shallows & the frogs have disappeared.

Infirmary for a Private Soul

RECIPE FOR S&M MARMALADE

Blood oranges
should be eaten
blushing,
cupped
in the palm.
   Easily entered
fingers
separate skin from flesh
carefully pulling
segment by segment
opening the ruby-orange
rosy-wet.

Ignore the rest,
         the bitter Sevilles,
         the Hamlins,
         the under-ripe
         green-tinged,
         the rusty orange.
         Mottled.
         Rough.
         Sour.

Leave them
to the flash
of a newly whetted blade,
sharp and cold
cutting into skin and flesh.
  Slice.
  Soak.
Turn up heat,
boil until flesh melts

& blisters
thick deep orange.

Think only of the end,
the mouth-feel,
the stew of dark sweet,
& juice,
& thickened pulp
    you swallow.

Infirmary for a Private Soul

MEDIUM RARE

The farmyard fence, chickens,
beyond, a grazing herd.
Think warm, think brown, think white.

*

Think sirloin, think skirt steak.
Saignant, blood pooling
in rivulets under potatoes,
the mica-glint of fat globules.

A Sauce Piquant spooned over slices
& then a surfeit of grease.

*

Say *hen,* say *egg,* say *moo.*
The menu says the meat
                     is killed humanely.
The tabletop's a little high,
brown steer hide pulled tight,
(fatty female said to be the cruelest cut
also the most tender.)

*

Steer hide on the tabletop,
pulled tight. Skin-thin
lamp shades.
Fat globules. Soap.

*

The farmyard fence, chickens, goats,
beyond, a grazing herd.
Please stand tall now,
the steer and cow are standing
taller than you—& they're walking our way.

*

In Waziristan near the mountains
soldier Lars from Iowa
now barely nineteen
(he said *hen*   said *egg*   said *moo)*—
captured, beheaded.

*

I swallow,
you swallow,
we swallow.

Think sirloin, think skirt steak.
Our bill handed to us
the way bills always are.

Infirmary for a Private Soul

JENIN, PALESTINE

April 2002

Because of what happened here,
because of what did not happen,
the soldiers move from house to house
in the densely peopled camp.
I know that camp. Many things don't
go on as they did, but a few do.

Only a few know what to do
because of what happened here.
Soldiers and the people don't
feed their dogs now. It could happen
again. How many in the camp
used to have a goat, a house,

a place to call their own? Housed
in lean-tos, how many still do?
The scraping of a pot in camp
scatters the pigeons. Over there
a chicken scratches for seeds that happen
to lie around the rubble. *Don't,*

someone said, *Careful, don't
touch anything in the house.*
One remembered what could happen:
walls falling, not knowing what to do
because of the confusion here
and what had swept through the camp.

How many may have stayed in camp
no one knows but those who don't
turn up—well, concrete's here
instead, just rumors where a house
had been. Those who do
turn up sweep, stack. Some happen

to actually hear those buried alive. It happens.
Rumors? Well, they may be true. In camp
either way people do
know who's gone. They don't
listen to officials checking the house
(or whatever's left of it here)

who ask, *What happened?* They don't
answer in the camp, but the houses
only concrete shells, speak here.

Summer Hunger

A JEW IN THE CUPBOARD

for Tadeus Rosewicz

The weather is uncertain out
and inside too as in Poland
after the war.

We talk of Rozewicz renaming
his world: *This is a tree, a goat.*
This is the rebirth

of spring, a leaf, a man
a woman, whole
after the winter.

Right here drivers move through
an underpass, avert their eyes
to avoid men sleeping,

look away from women
shadowed in doorways.
One, nose bleeding hard,

runs to a doctor. *A Walk-in*
the nurse calls out. *An Ankle's on the phone
but we don't do ankles here either.*

Rozewicz might say
This is a shoe, a bar of soap,
This is a ring, a suitcase.

What would you do
if threatened? Would you
point to the cupboard?

A man, a woman small as a dish.
In a closet a person
can stand tall, hiding.

In a cupboard
an object rests. A small Jew
in uncertain weather.

Summer Hunger

CONVERSATIONS WITH BASHO, BUSON & SOSEKI

Even in Kyoto—
hearing the cuckoo's cry—
I long for Kyoto.

Basho

京にても京なつかしや時鳥

Even at dawn dreams & daylight marry
in a Murakami world. Our spirit-words walk
Kyoto silently. Yes, & at dusk we tread lightly.
Hearing footsteps might make us disappear.
The past lives inside us here on Shinmonzendori. A
cuckoo's voice calls from the clockshop. No hawkers
cry out, only the shuffle of shoppers' shoes—& mine.
I am comfort, I sway under my silks,
long to sing chansons, speak French with the French.
For twenty years I have poured tea, danced, imitated pleasure.
Kyoto, my prison.

A Cumulus Fiction

Light of the moon
moves west, flowers' shadows
creep eastward.

Buson

月
光
西
に
わ
た
れ
ば
花
影
東
に
歩
む
か
な

Light at night sees the unseen, underbellies
of rocks, a scramble of millipedes & sowbugs.
The paralyzing exposure. A full
moon paints Rothko on the meadow, blueblack & dancing,
moves the insects from chaos to choreography.
West of the field salt & ocean spray, a lone
flower's mist and bloom. The shadow of
shadows. Deep purples, blackgreens vibrate,
creep into the dim field. Wait—look
eastward—orange light is tricking the night.

A Cumulus Fiction

The crow has flown away:
swaying in the evening sun,
a leafless tree.

Soseki

烏
飛
ん
で
夕
日
に
動
く
冬
木
か
な

The gate here rings bells to scare off
crow or jay, an uninvited guest. What
has been an early warning
flown awry is meant to keep
away intruders. Frighten them.
Swaying—the slightest movement
in the air wakes up the night. Cowbells.
The triangle. A tambourine. But wait, there's
evening music if you listen, a play of light like
sun at midnight sets off your noonday heat.
A wind sings a symphony. No silent
leafless limbs hang. Bells ring. Not a
tree at all, & once I thought you were ordinary.

A Cumulus Fiction

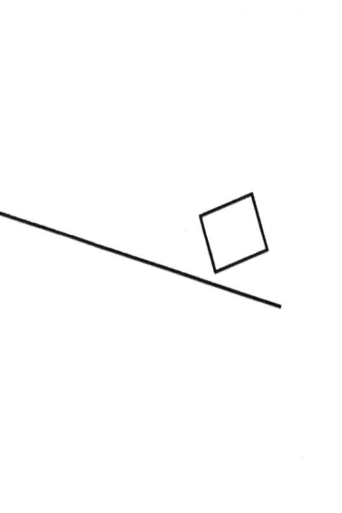

TO A FOSSIL

Olduvai Gorge, Tanzania, 1959

Hide and seek,
a run under palm frond canopies.
After someone like me must have drowsed
on jackal pelts, you rank with sweat,
steaming, four arms, four legs tangled,
listening in the yellow-eyed dark
for the crackle of a step from the streambed
where rivercresses grow.

You slept away millennia
in sediment with hare and fish and bird,
once carrion of the hawk
circling above. Even now
he eyes the rifted gorge. Spies your jaw.
You, blood to stone to hand, my hand
that pulls you speechless
from the hot earth.

Summer Hunger

PECH MERLE

Listen history,
a hand print found
washes time away.

Your voice,
the sound you uttered
pressing palm
fingers to stone
talks to me of arms
like my own.

Say you know my warmth
and mean to greet
your child whose hand fits yours,
who hears you speak.

Summer Hunger

INFIRMARY FOR A PRIVATE SOUL

exquisite order
           & space
outside/inside the bricks

soul says
    the examining room
    lives its own precision   exact doses
    exact
      too-tight boundaries

    the doors want light   glass

soul roams
through ward & nurse-room
invites noise
             kind kitchen chatter

longs for the scent
of melted butter browning

longs for
singing   anyone singing

Infirmary for a Private Soul

SUMMER HUNGER, NEW YORK CITY

Start with the flat roof
where soot crackles under leather soles,
where pigeons peck crusts that wind lifts
over the parapet, necks jerking, faces turning
one way, the other, like windup toys
searching, waiting for a breadcrumb-dream,
as black grit drifts over tarpaper softened
from heat, days of heat pressed into granite,
into skin and skull, past bones to where
the sun scours cool reason away.

We set beach towels end to end,
let the rays toast one side, then the other,
turn our girlish reveries
to the Beauty of the Boyfriend, practice
the fluttering hand, the cinched waist,
imagine the rustle of a patterned skirt
all leaves and roses swaying just so at the hem,
consumed by what might
(it could you know   anytime now)
blow over the parapet.

Summer Hunger

ON GIVING A SILVER FOX PIECE
TO JESSICA

Because
    no one
        wears real fur in school,

because
        animal rights people stop you
            & make rude—

                        do you blame them?

Anyway
        the *vulpes vulpes* coat
        is glossy, warm
        enough to withstand
        the wildest wind,
        even sideways sleet, cool
        enough (a gift of comfort)
        in a shaded thicket.

                The silver fox in the wild is monogamous.
                The fox's habits are typically cautious.

        Droplets from a stream he fords
            glisten,
            slide off his oiled pelt.

            Following each mating period
            both parents raise their young.

    So who in conscience could wear real fur,

& besides I

    don't have anything it goes with—
                although

    around the neck it does flatter.

            Infirmary for a Private Soul

PARKING LOT NEAR SOUTH BROAD AND PASSYUNK IN JANUARY, PHILADELPHIA

Stripped thin.

Poplars. Blacktop.
Conspirators, splayed feet rooted
in rusted earth under snow.

Forget the mercies of summer,
the open laughter,
        how shadowplay
erases the self,
        how trees' lush shade
offers refuge,

only remember how
    the beating sun pounds asphalt,
    offers no mercy, how
    heat twists us like
    a buckled mirror teases & contorts.

Cold days like this turn you inside out,

fill crevices, puddle craters, shudder
under a sky that somehow embraces
even this sordid lot
its abandoned cars,

        & we float somewhere
                        inbetween

            wary of gusts
that shiver the gun-metal
clouds in glassy wet.

            In the distance the lowing
of cumulus thunder. Come stand with me
here at the edge of the end,
where weather stops dead, color
dissolves.
            This disconnect.
            This falling.

Infirmary for a Private Soul

WEATHER

three *bouts-rimes*

This is the month air spits out June,
pretty June of the freight train's roar, of stress
churning funnel-like—June of the placid moon
staring blank-faced down inside. Winds obsess,
weave in and out. Think of a basket, snake
on snake, a nest of vipers writhing. Moot,
the celebration of who lives—cake
is icing, taste is life itself. *A beaut,*
the sucked up voice vanishes like a Garbo
smile, like the Listener in Beckett's play.
Air twists the wrung-out rags of clouds, takes a hobo,
takes the nursing infant's mother. Gone, as day
turns coal, as Death taunts, shakes his rhinestone
scepters, reeks of grim cologne.

                    *

But something's turned on edge—just see what June
inflicts on hot July, expectation? Stress?
No -- though something steals the August moon.
The hour's dusk and we obsess
again on what to eat, coil snake-
enjambed, limb on limb. Dessert is moot
now that we're filled, devouring (cake-
like) each other. I read your skin, read *beaut*
as beaut-iful, the aftertaste of sweet. Garbo
can have *Alone, Alone,* her game, her play.
You, haunches swinging under your hobo
chic, make Sunday every day.
You, facets dancing from a rhinestone,
scent the air with new-mown hay's cologne.

                    *

Yes, for the poet any day in June
will do. A bud's soft green or even stress
can birth a sonnet, say, about the moon,
poor beleaguered over-written moon. Obsess
and write, obsess and write—or snake
through both to dream of blue. Moot
again the swirling winds, bouts-rimes not scanned, no cake-
walk here—but give it time. *Beaut*
I start and cross it out, think of Garbo,
of her mask, her barely smile, play
with exhausted words, tie them as a hobo
ties his clothes with rope. Is this a sonnet day
I wonder, a day to write the yellow rhinestone white?
To wander, slant-rhyme roam, cologne?

Summer Hunger

PRAISE SMALL THINGS

Red clay tradebeads in a dreadlock braid,
the scent of earth-musk after rain,
a cicada chorale shrieking in the sun,
the summer's chalky grass, oak-black shade.
Praise the sticky pollen on the bee's
hind legs, the blossom's private parts, the fruit.
Praise all vowels: *masa* and *metate,*
smooth and *avocado, quesadilla.*
Praise Nomo backing first base on Beltre's throw,
Cohen reaching Ahmed, Ahmed reaching
words both used to know, speaking, speaking.
Praise the wild geese rising slow,
circling after rain to taste the scent
of air, of earth, this earth.

Summer Hunger

NOTES

NEW POEMS

ANOTHER NEW POEM (page 7)
After Charles Wright's *The New Poem:*

> It will not resemble the sea.
> It will not have dirt on its thick hands.
> It will not be part of the weather.
>
> It will not reveal its name.
> It will not have dreams you can count on.
> It will not be photogenic.
>
> It will not attend our sorrow.
> It will not console our children.
> It will not be able to help us.

ABE, THE TILE MAN (page 9)
The crooked straight and the rough places plain
from Handel's *The Messiah,*
It is Enough from Mendelssohn's *The Elijah*

THE VOICE OF THE FROG (page 10)
"Something we were withholding made us weak / Until we found out it was ourselves." From *The Gift Outright,* Robert Frost.

"What took me / completely by surprise / was that it was me: / my voice, in my mouth. / Without thinking at all / I was my foolish aunt." From *In the Waiting Room,* Elizabeth Bishop

BBC SHIPPING FORECAST, FACING SOUTH (page 12)
Phrases lifted from the BBC's Shipping News Forecast; the concept "facing" from Frank Bidart's "making" in *Music Like Dirt.* I played with the poem and the idea as though in a Pantoum.

ON CONSCIENCE (page 13)
Three triolets. Each is a poem of eight lines, typically of eight syllables, that rhymes: *abaaabab*. It is structured so that the first line recurs as the fourth and seventh and the second as the eighth. Originally French, mid 17th century.

PORTRAIT (page 16)
Osmel Sousa, longtime head of the Miss Venezuela pageant, on the popularity of plastic surgery in Venezuela. (*NY Times*, 11.9.13).
The phrase *in a convex mirror* after John Ashbery.

DEPENDING ON THE YEAR (page 17)
A broken pantoum. First and last lines from the poem *"Dear Rose"* from *Time is a Mother* by Ocean Vuong.

DEPRESSION SOUP, 1936 (page 18)
In Palmistry *mount of moon,* an area at the base of the palm opposite the thumb, said to be the source of creativity, moods & emotions. *Mount of Venus,* opposite the mount of moon said to be the source of energy, love, affection and sympathy.

ABOUT CHARGED BODIES (page 20)
"The world of the subjunctive", a line *from Worms* by Carl Dennis
Earthing busbars establish security and act as conductors of electrical current.

FABLE ON ERASURE (page 30)
Fable of Fables, Nazim Hikmet; poems of Nazim Hikmet, Persea Books, 2002. A meditation on encroaching political pressures in Russia and in the states of Florida and Texas.

SELECTED POEMS

CORE BALANCE TRAINER (page 39)
Portions taken from the Hammacher Schlemmer Catalog, Spring 2007.

WATERVILLE, MAINE, NEAR GREAT POND (page 41)
The Brazilian Poet Carlos Drummond de Andrade ends his post-World War I poem, *Souvenir of the Ancient World*, with these prescient words: *They had gardens, they had mornings in those days!*

SIDEWINDER (page 48)
Lines 17 and 18 from James Wright's poem "Moon" (*Above the River: the Complete Poems* by James Wright, Farrar, Straus & Giroux, NY 1992) "*And I will give you / My life, my own . . .*"

———

THE DREAM (page 54)
I don't love you as if you were salt-rose or topaz, from Pablo Neruda's *100 Love Sonnets (Cien Sonetos de Amor)*, University of Texas Press, Austin, 1986.

———

JENIN, PALESTINE (page 70)
From accounts of the Israeli military incursion into Janin, April 14, 2002; Rick Bragg reported in the *NY Times*, April 15, 2002.

———

CONVERSATIONS WITH BASHO, BUSON & SOSEKI (page 75)
My responses to the haiku masters own poems (haikus). These three interactions are from my chapbook *A Cumulus Fiction* (Finishing Line Press, 2019).

———

INFIRMARY FOR A PRIVATE SOUL (page 81)
After the watercolor "Infirmary for a Private School" by architect Carlos
Leonhauser for the Atelier of the San Francisco Architecture Club, 1914.
"Soul Says,"essays by Helen Vendler, her title after Jorie Graham's poem
"Soul Says."

ON GIVING A SILVER FOX PIECE TO JESSICA (page 83)
Italicized portions describing the Silver Fox excerpted from Wikipedia.

WEATHER (page 86)
The poem is composed of three bouts-rimes, an old French parlor game in
which players are given end rhymes and must compose a verse, usually a
sonnet, using them in the order given; the more peculiar the end rhymes the
greater the challenge. Instead of the sonnet form I used the sestina.
The Listener and *The Reader*, two impassive characters in Samuel Becket's
"Ohio Impromptu."

ACKNOWLEDGMENTS

My thanks to the journals below for publishing my work:

Beyond Baroque Literary Arts Center Poetry Contest, "Medium Rare"
Georgia Poetry Society Contest (first place), "Undelivered Mother's Day"
Just a Little More Time, anthology, "Spider"
Nimrod International Journal, Four Poems from *A Cumulus Fiction*
Ploughshares, "A Violence of Season"
Pratik, a Magazine of Contemporary Literature, "Circle" (chosen by the editor
    to preface the volume)
Runes (Arctos Press), "A Jew in the Cupboard"
Solo, "The Dream"
The Gastronomic Reader Anthology, "Recipe for S&M Marmalade"
The Ginosko Literary Journal, a folio of 11 poems from *Precarious*
Tor House Prize for Poetry (third place), "Waterville Maine near Great Pond"
Universal Oneness (Authorspress, New Delhi), "Bird"
Verse Daily, "Kin"

Gratitude can hardly describe my thanks to David St. John, Dorothy Barresi, Richard Garcia and Gail Wronsky for the years of mentoring, teaching and enlarging my vision of what poetry can be. It is a privilege to have worked with them.

Heartfelt thanks also to my dear friends and workshop colleagues who have shared their knowledge and careful parsing of my work for more than twenty years: Brenda Yates, Beth Ruscio, Candace Pearson, Carine Topal, Cathie Sandstrom, Kate Hovey, Keven Bellows, Marjorie Becker, Mary Fitzpatrick, Lynne Thompson, and Kimberly Young. Every poem is improved by their consideration; their vision is here too on these pages.

And as for those first drafts and early readings—trial by fire—special thanks to my scorched but patient readers Magda Waingrow and Holaday Mason and to tolerant and equally patient Ken Fisher. He is the man who allows me time and space for this work to grow and is, as always, my heart and home.

REMEMBERING

the songs sung with my parents around the piano, Kipling's rhythm and assonance in *The Elephant's Child* (his "satiable curiosity" all too familiar); Jane Siegel's broad smile, sneakers hanging from her finger at the police station, her Vietnam War-time protest; Jerry Pacht's humor, wit and wisdom, his gorgeous baritone, his generosity. I remember my "brother" Elliot Elgart and the advice he freely gave—his hand, his art graces our home today; family meals and conversation with Vernie and Arthur Ourieff at their round table in the kitchen, dissecting poetry, and our trips to nether-lands in search of the perfect dim sum meal followed by another search (bogus) for nearby real estate. Many more, none forgotten.

JUDITH PACHT's book *Summer Hunger* won the 2011 PEN Southwest Book Award for Poetry. Recent poetry books are *Infirmary for a Private Soul* and *A Cumulus Fiction*. A three-time Pushcart nominee, Pacht was first place winner in the Georgia Poetry Society's Edgar Bowers competition. Her poem "KIN" was published recently on *Verse Daily*, and her work appears in numerous anthologies and journals such as *Ploughshares*, *Runes*, *Nimrod* and *Phoebe*. Her poetry has been translated into Russian and published in *Foreign Literature*, Moscow, Russia. Pacht reads at the Los Angeles Times Festival of Books, at Charleston's Piccolo Spoleto Festival, and she has read and taught Political Poetry at Denver's annual LitFest at the Lighthouse, at UCLA Extension, and at Beyond Baroque in Los Angeles.

www.ingramcontent.com/pod-product-compliance
Lightning Source LLC
Chambersburg PA
CBHW031441120626
46545CB00006B/2514